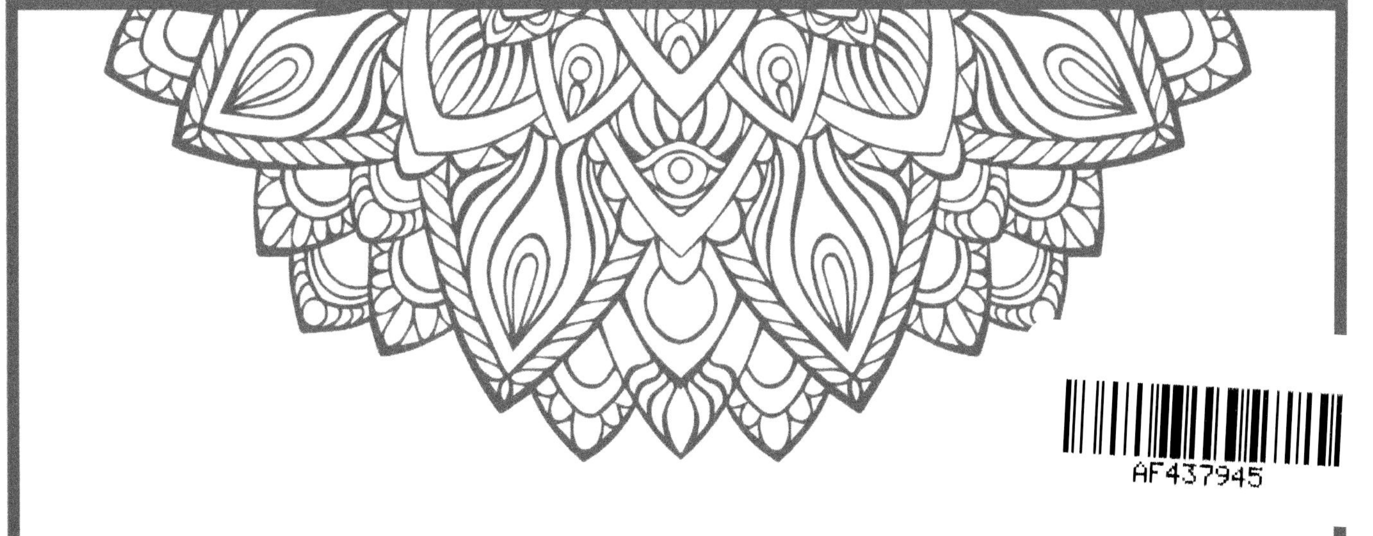

This Book Belongs To:

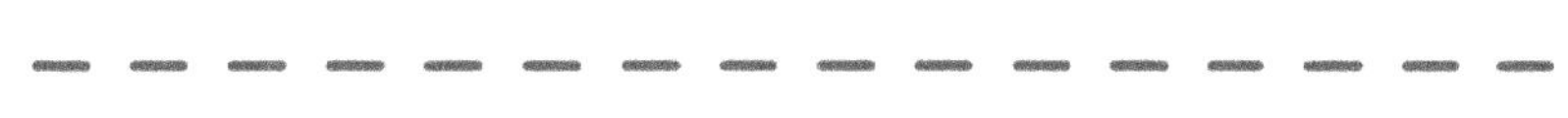

____

____

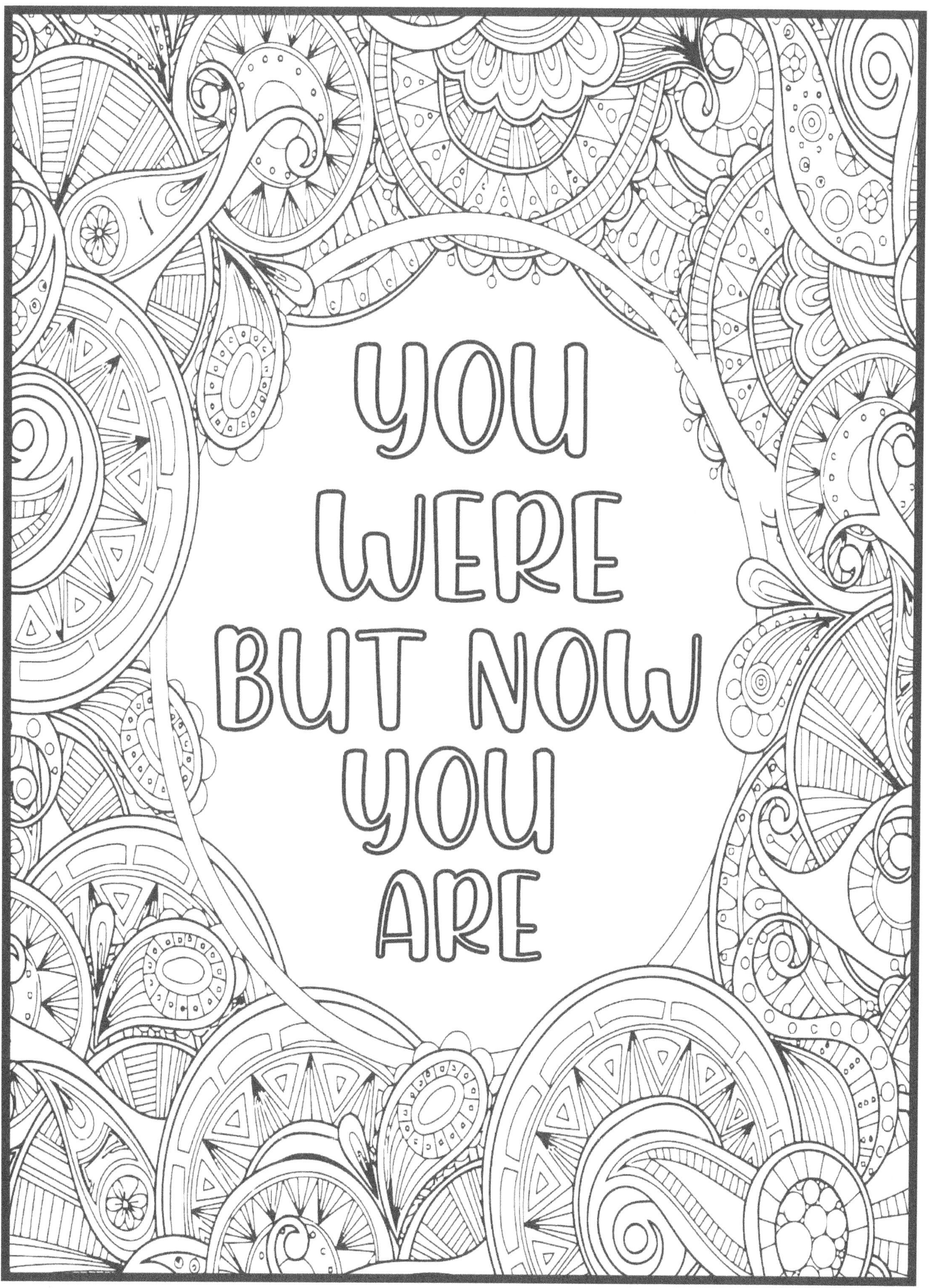

YOU
WERE
BUT NOW
YOU
ARE

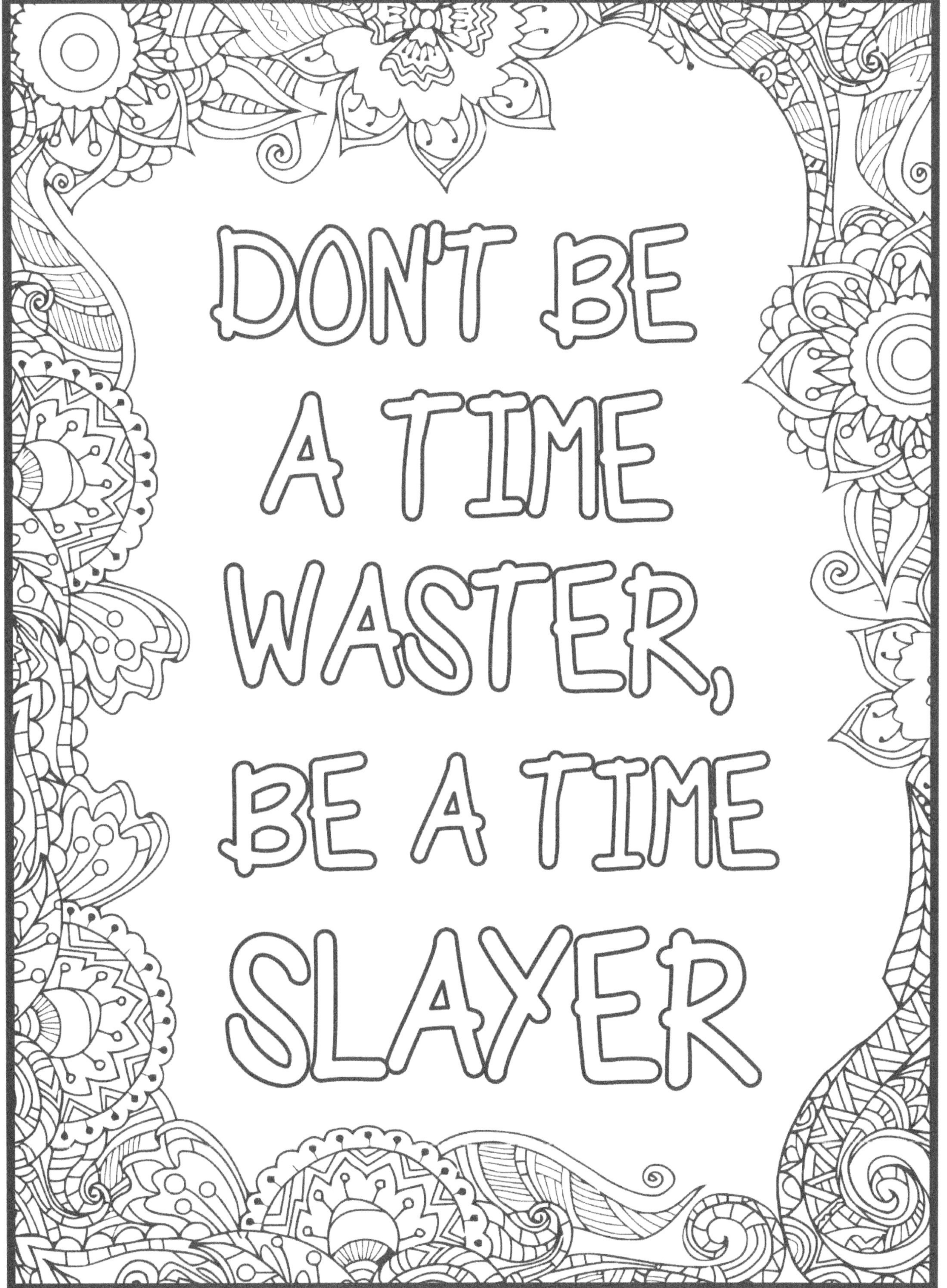

DON'T BE
A TIME
WASTER,
BE A TIME
SLAYER

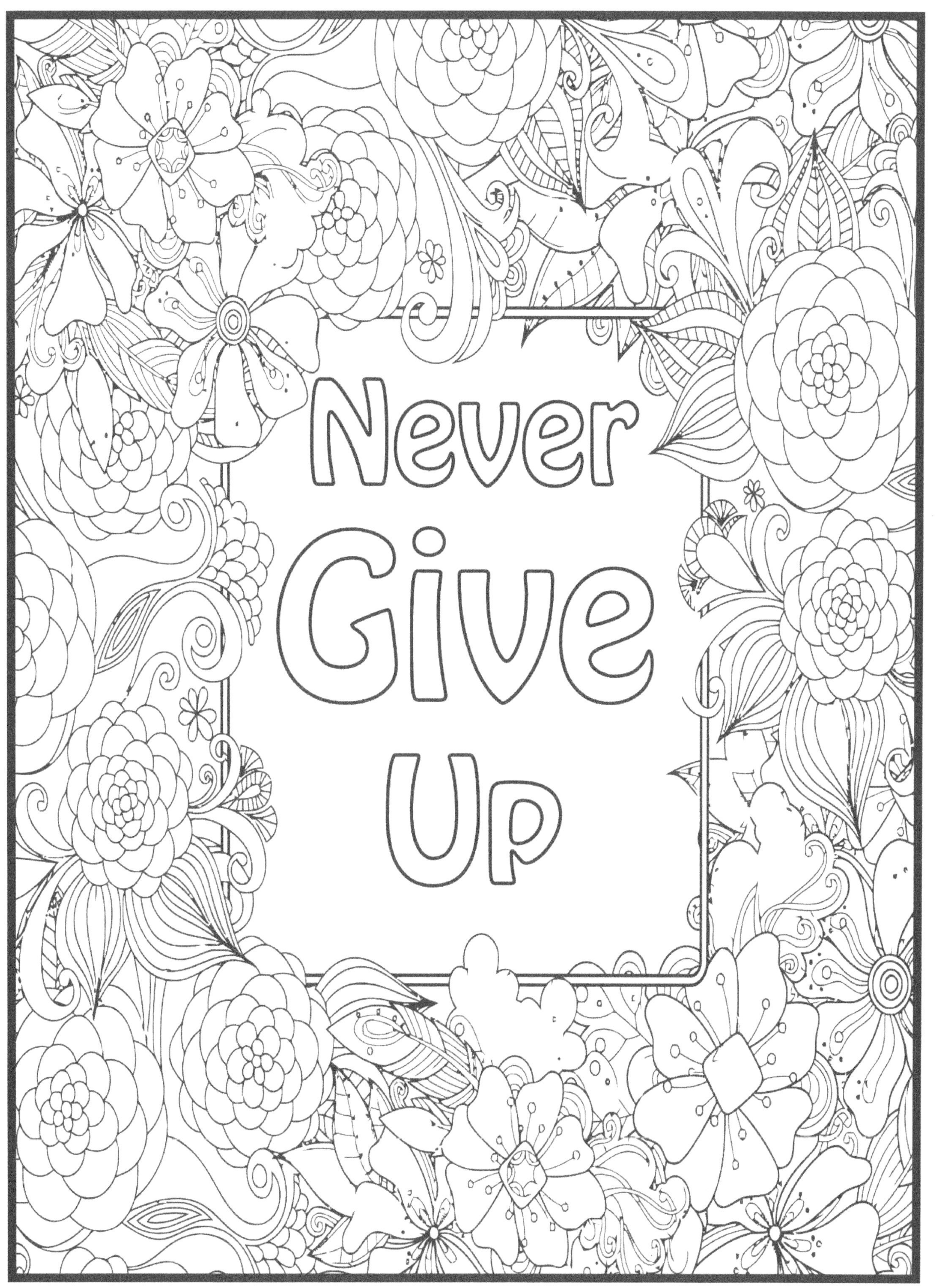

Never
Give
Up

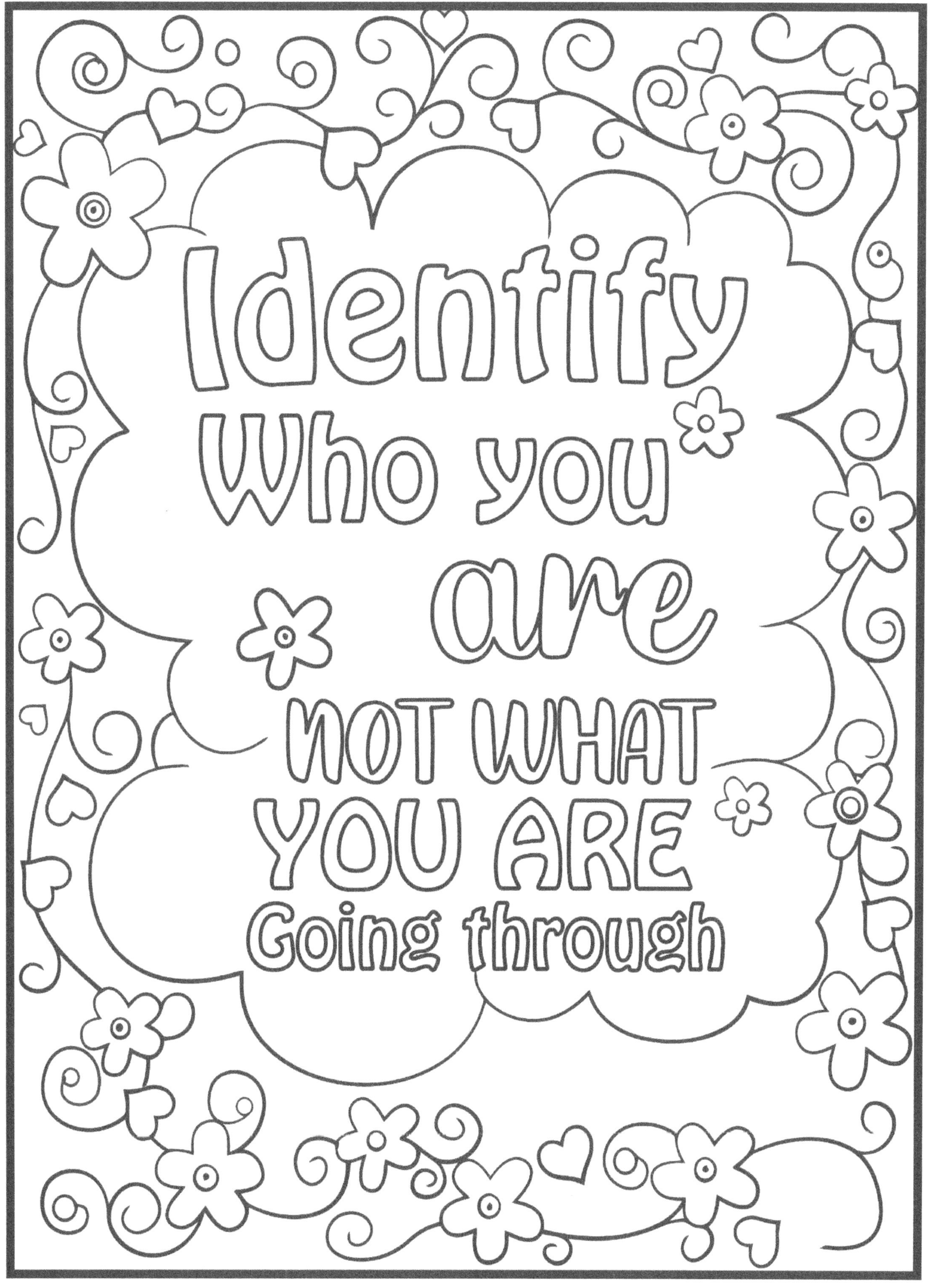

Identify
Who you
are
NOT WHAT
YOU ARE
Going through

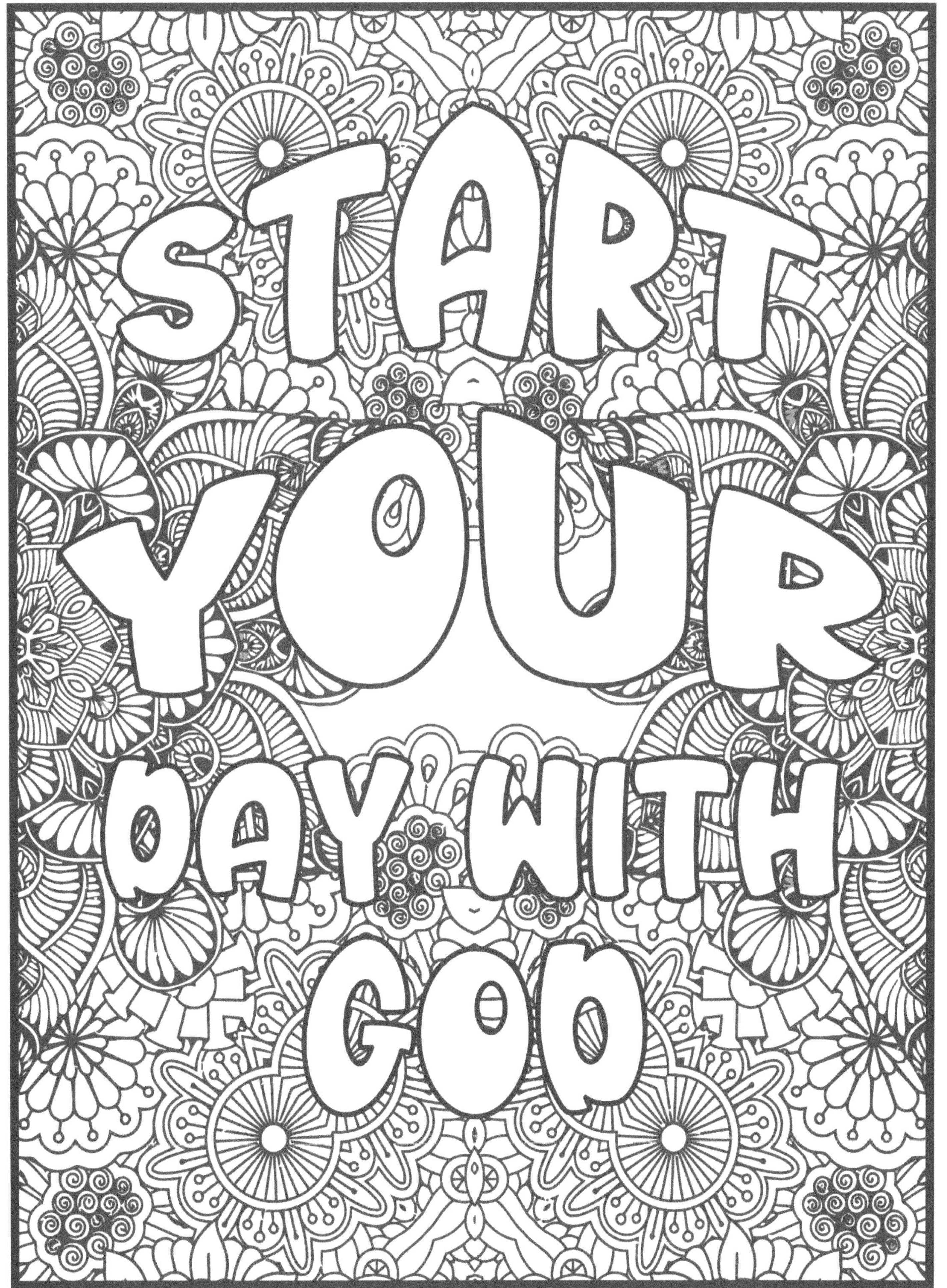

START
YOUR
DAY WITH
GOD

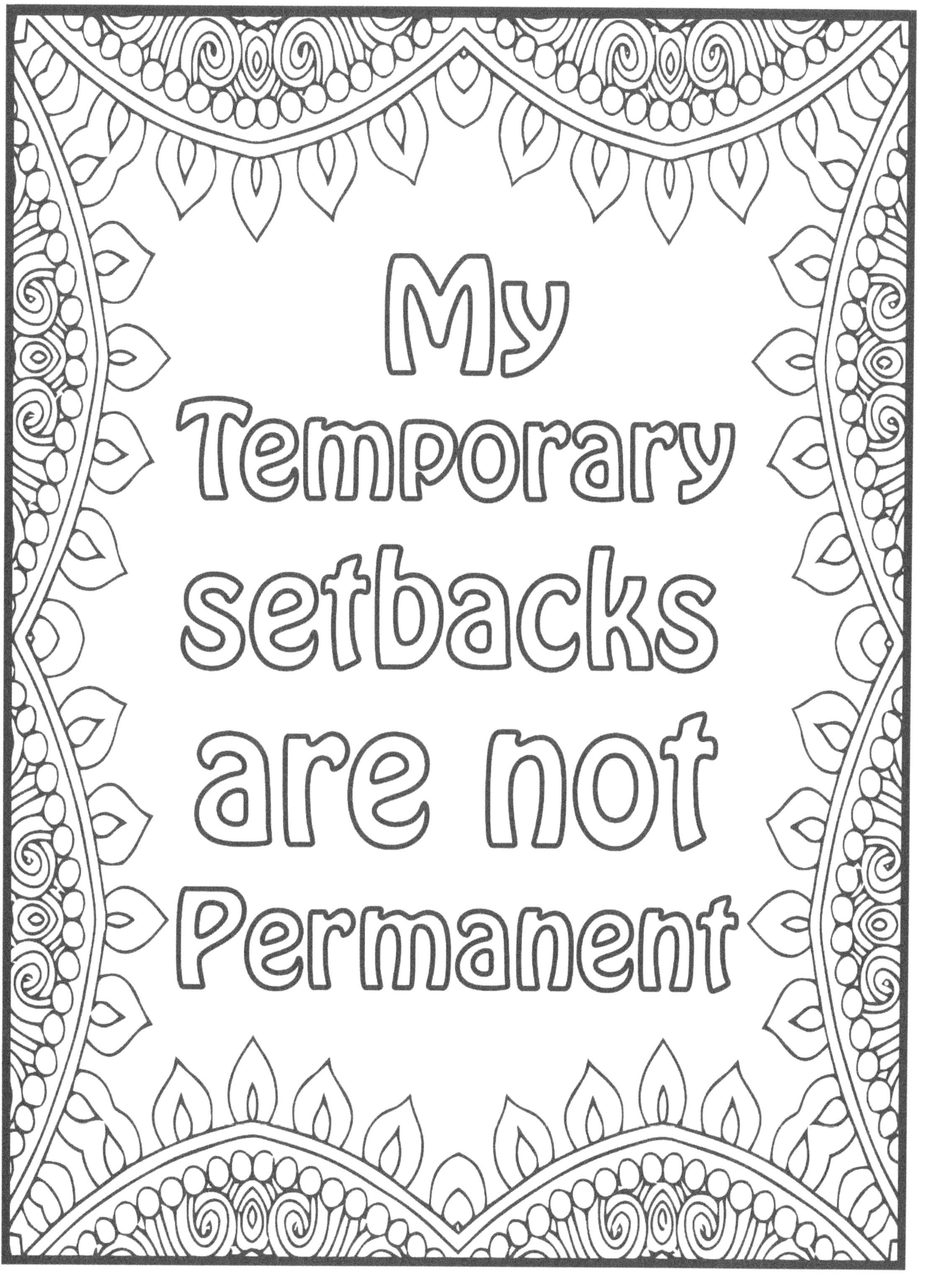

My
Temporary
setbacks
are not
Permanent

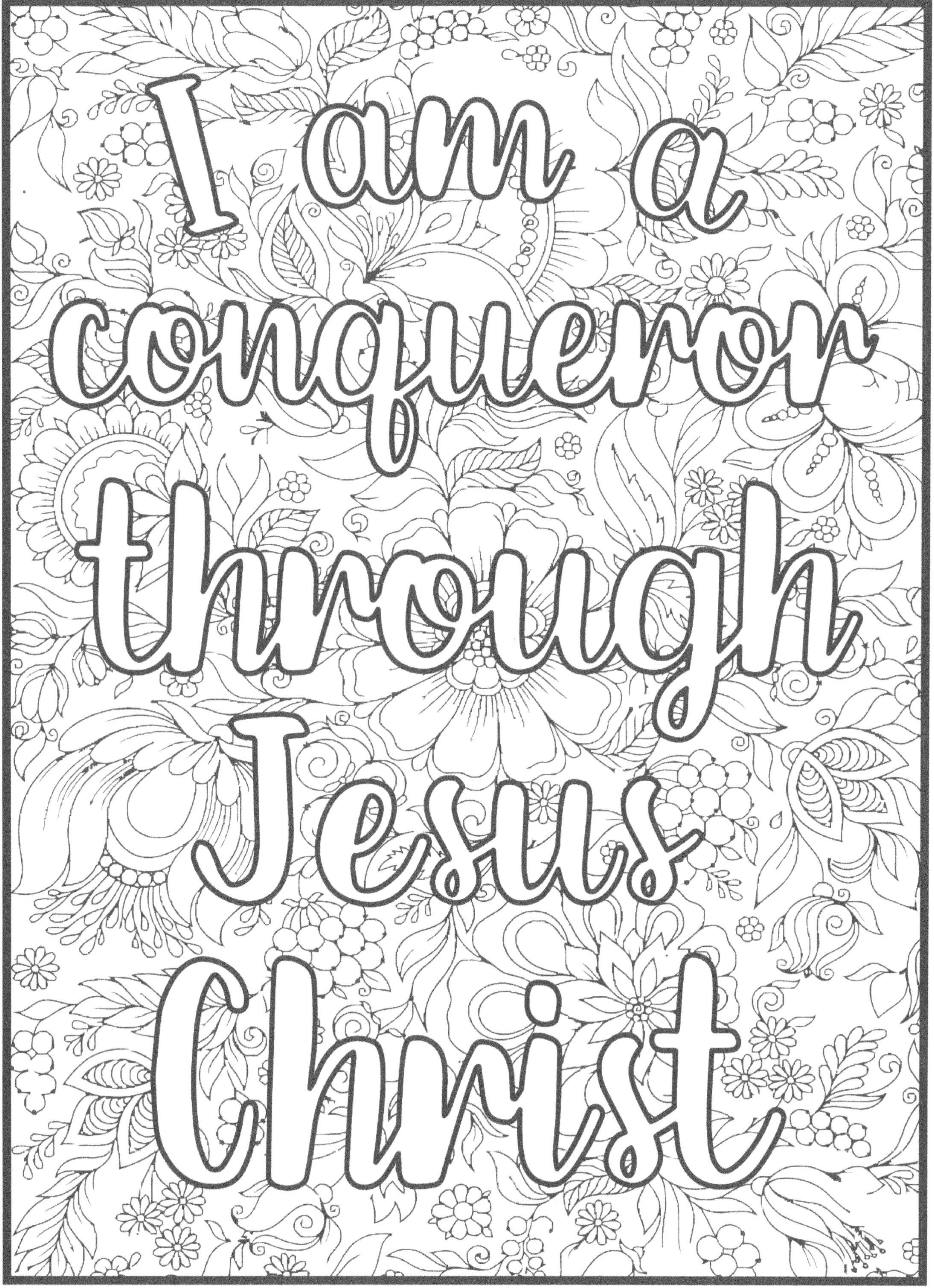
I am a
conqueror
through
Jesus
Christ

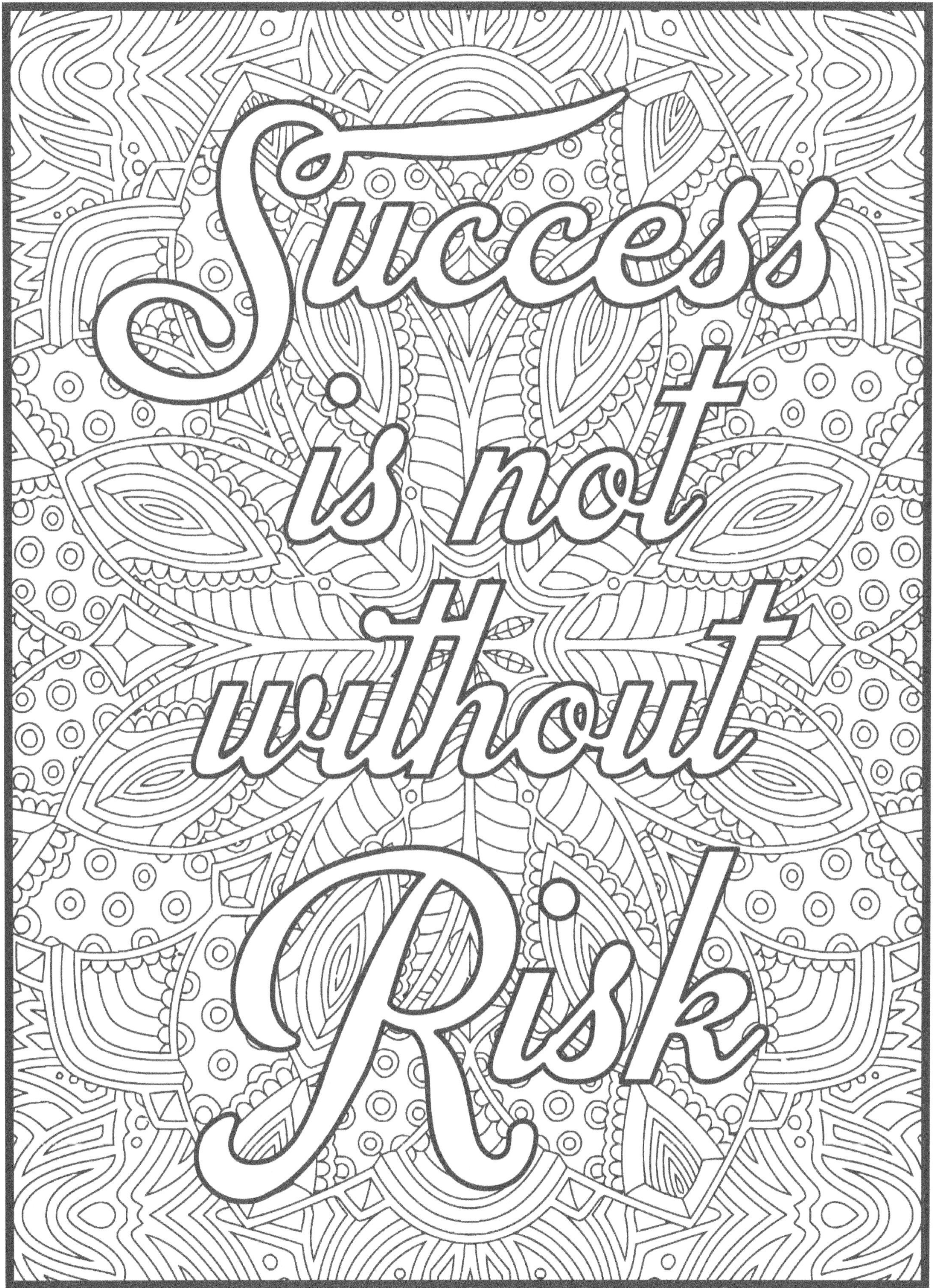
Success
is not
without
Risk

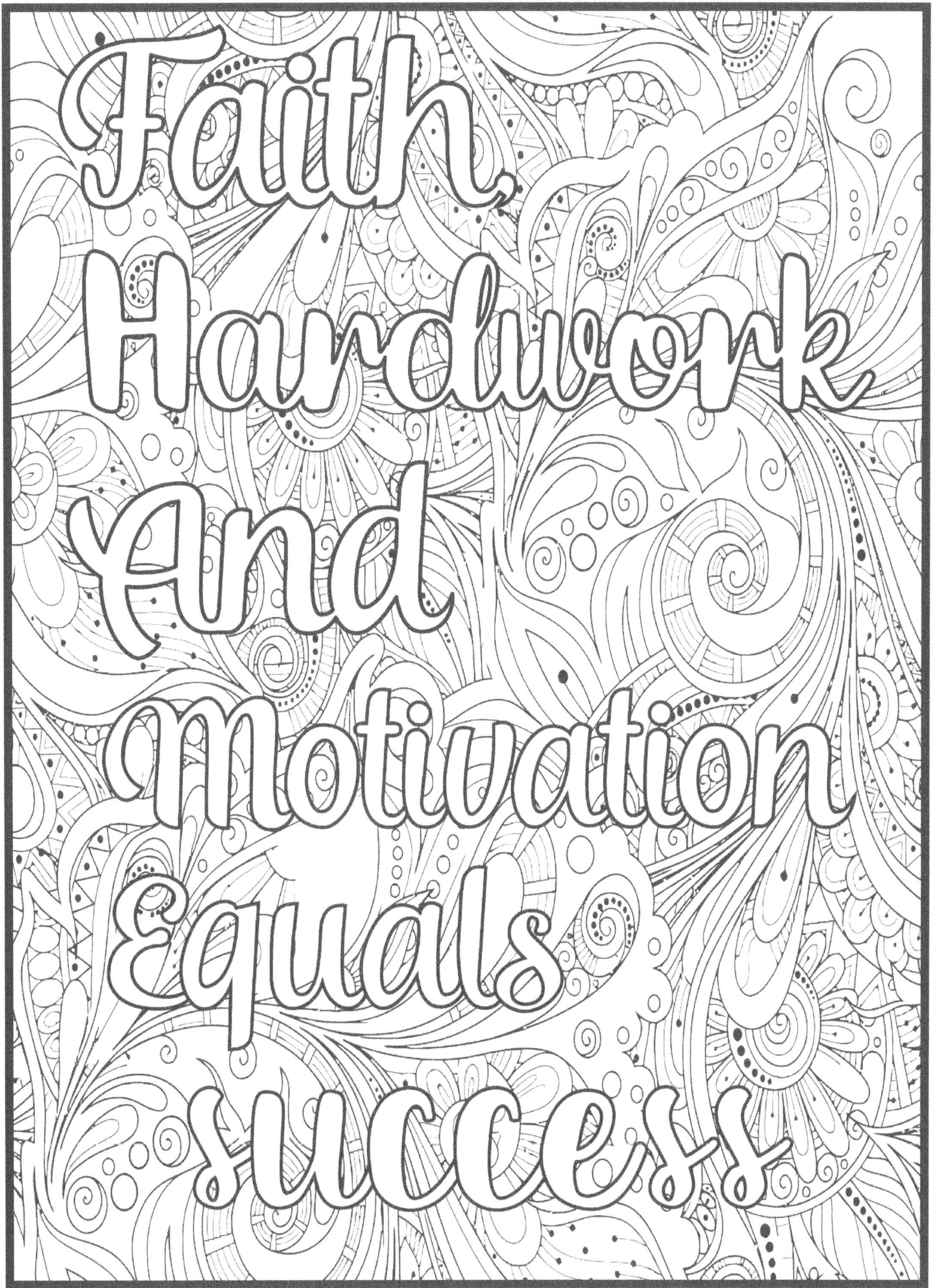

Faith,
Hardwork
And
Motivation
Equals
success

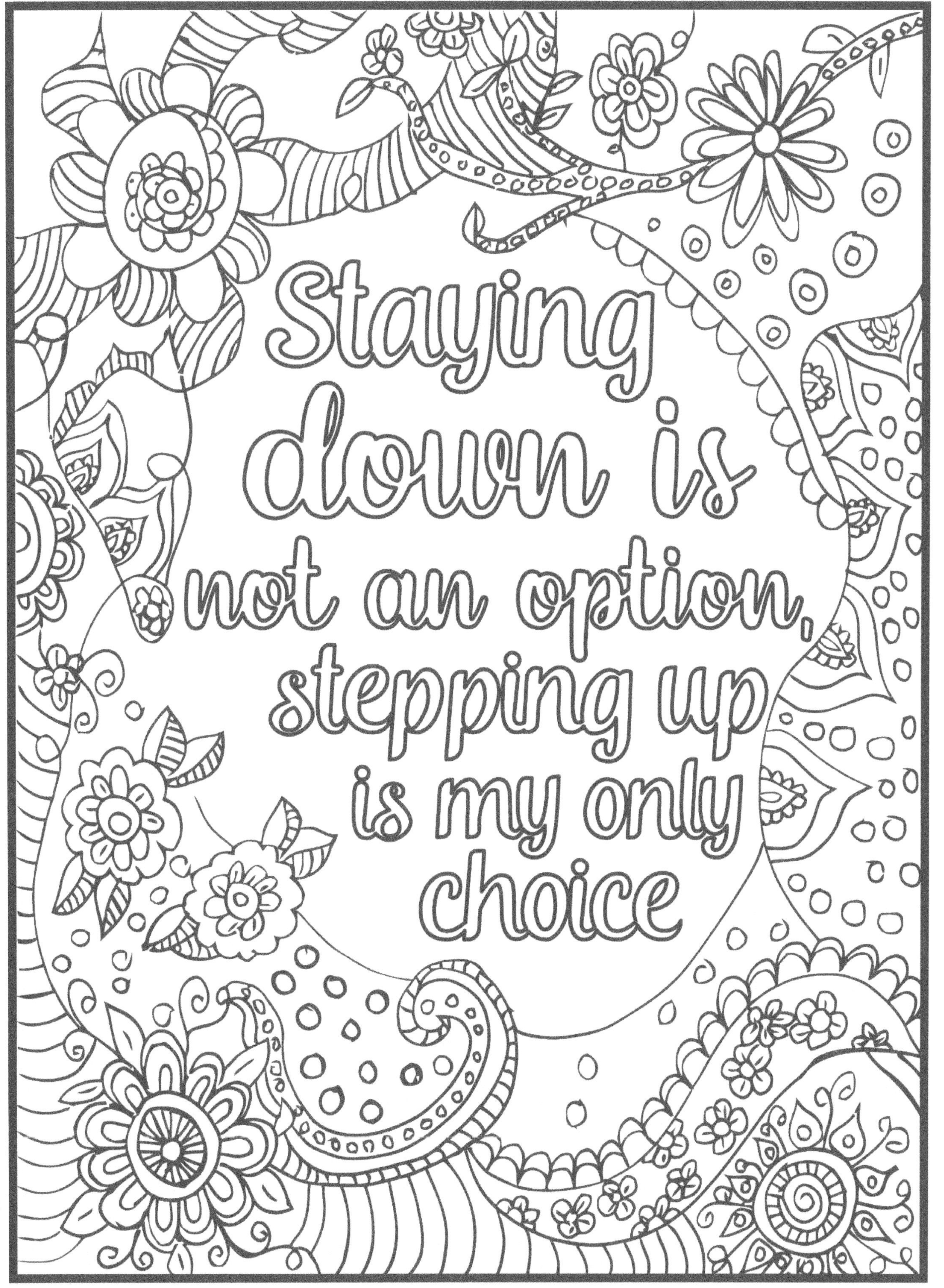
Staying
down is
not an option,
stepping up
is my only
choice

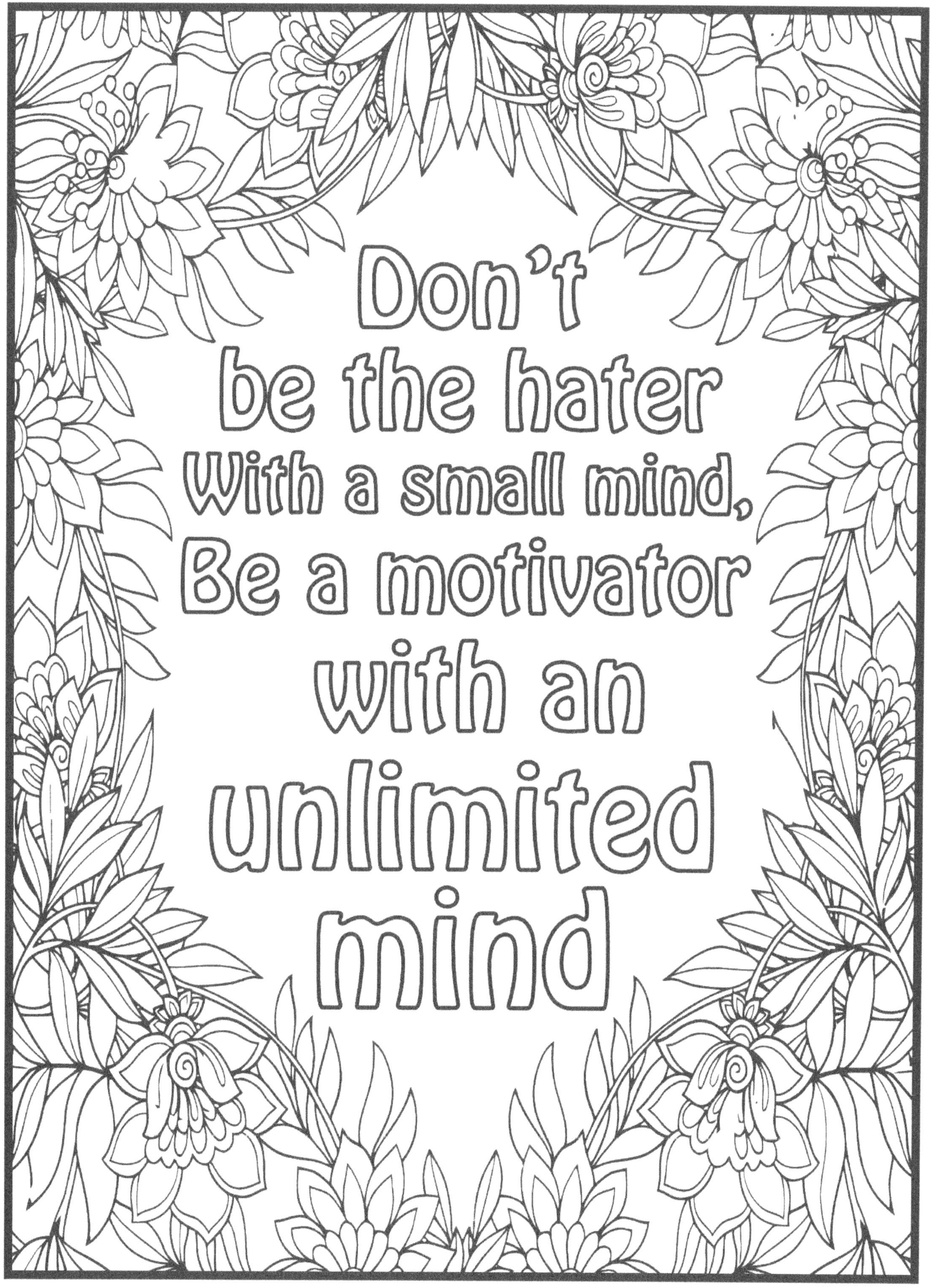

Don't
be the hater
With a small mind,
Be a motivator
with an
unlimited
mind

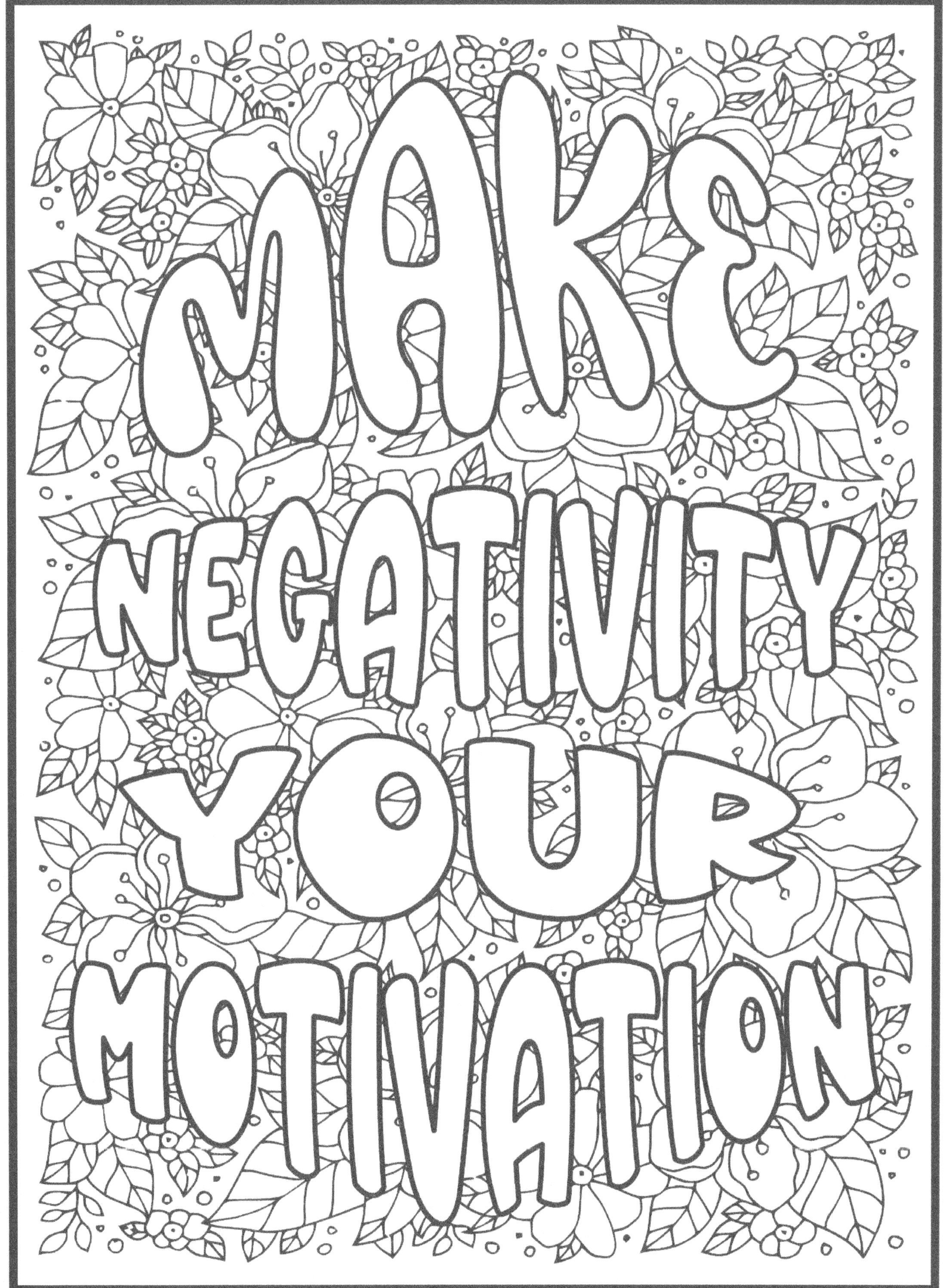

MAKE
NEGATIVITY
YOUR
MOTIVATION

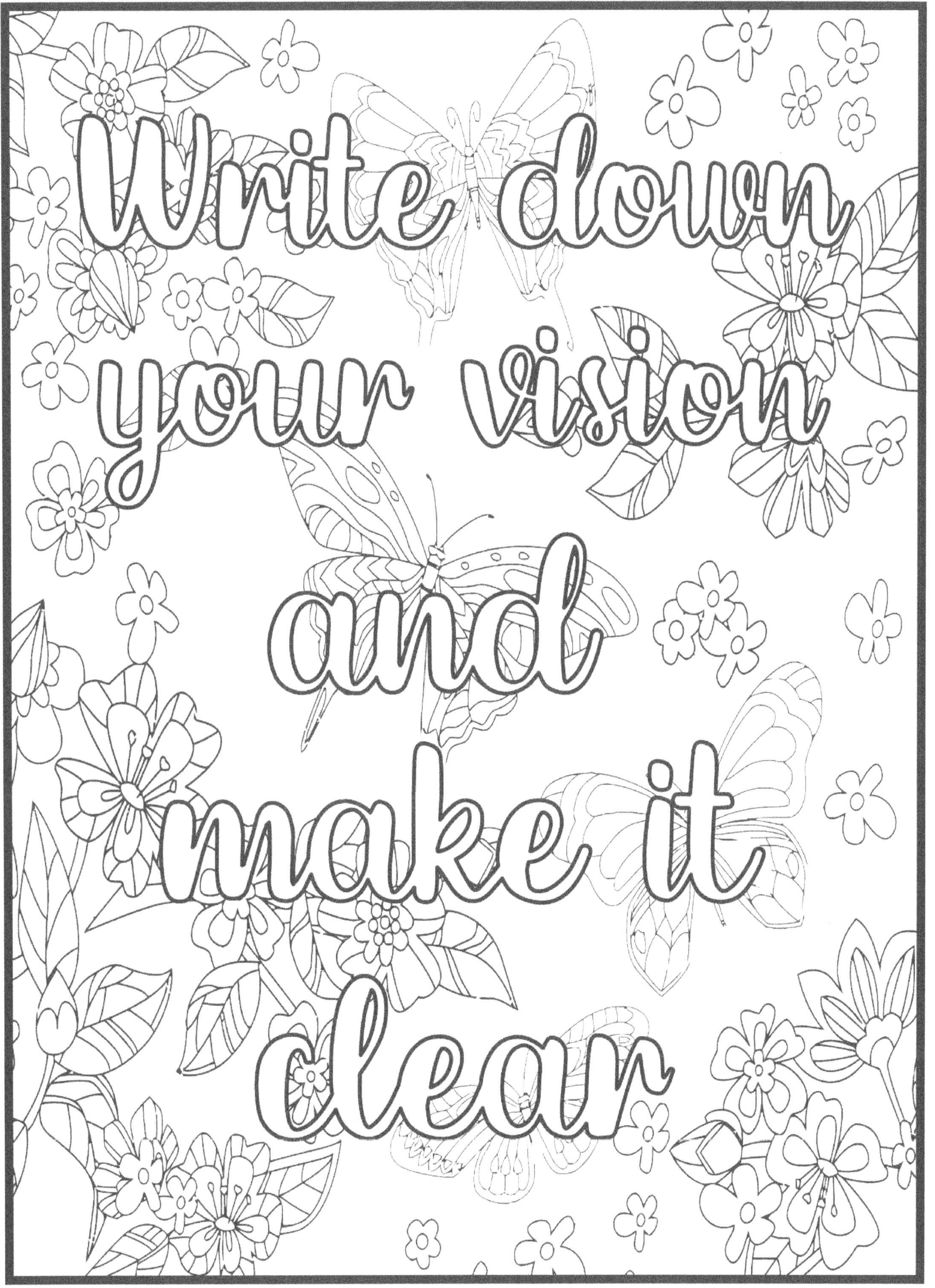

Write down
your vision
and
make it
clear

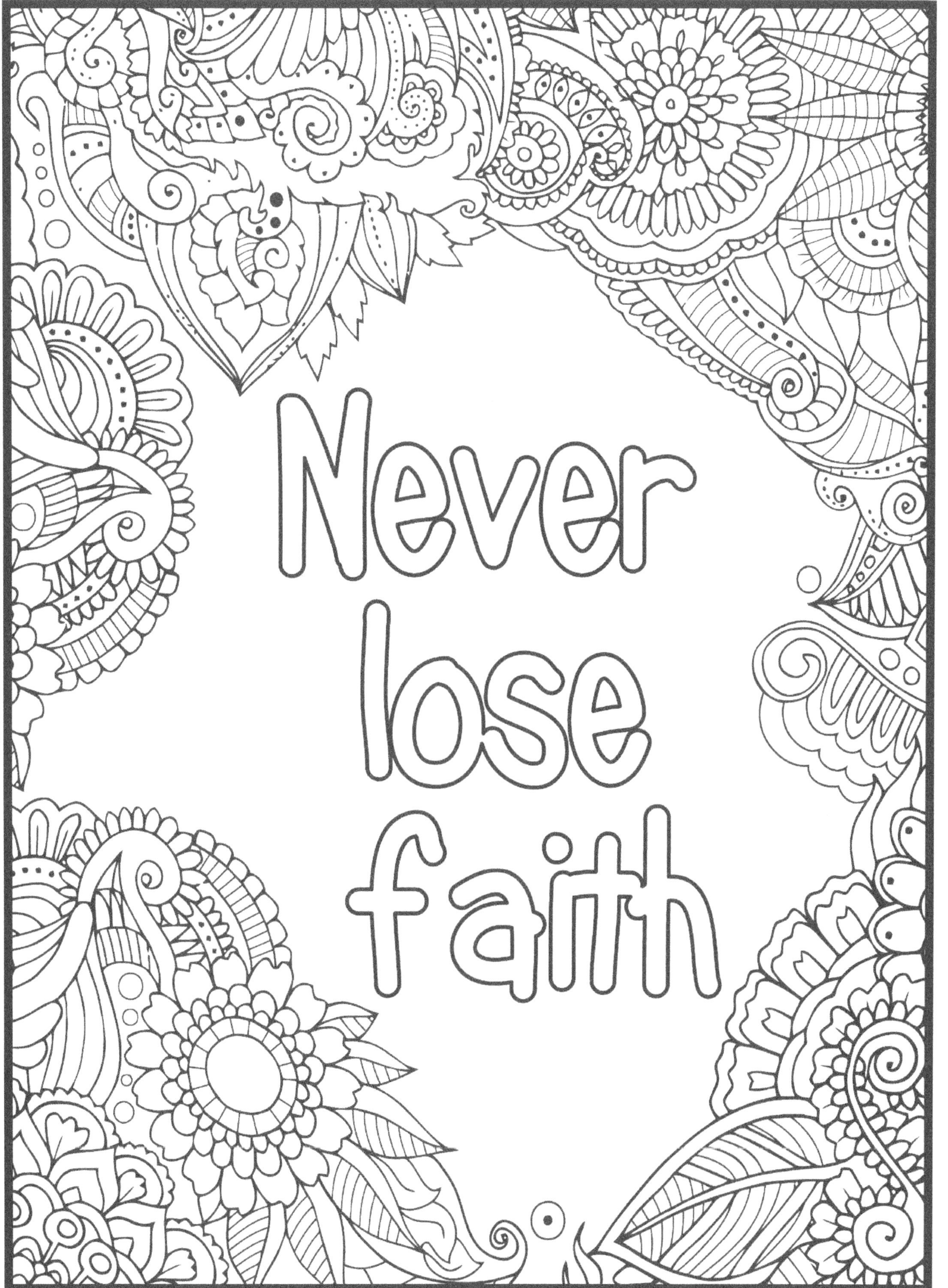

Never
lose
faith

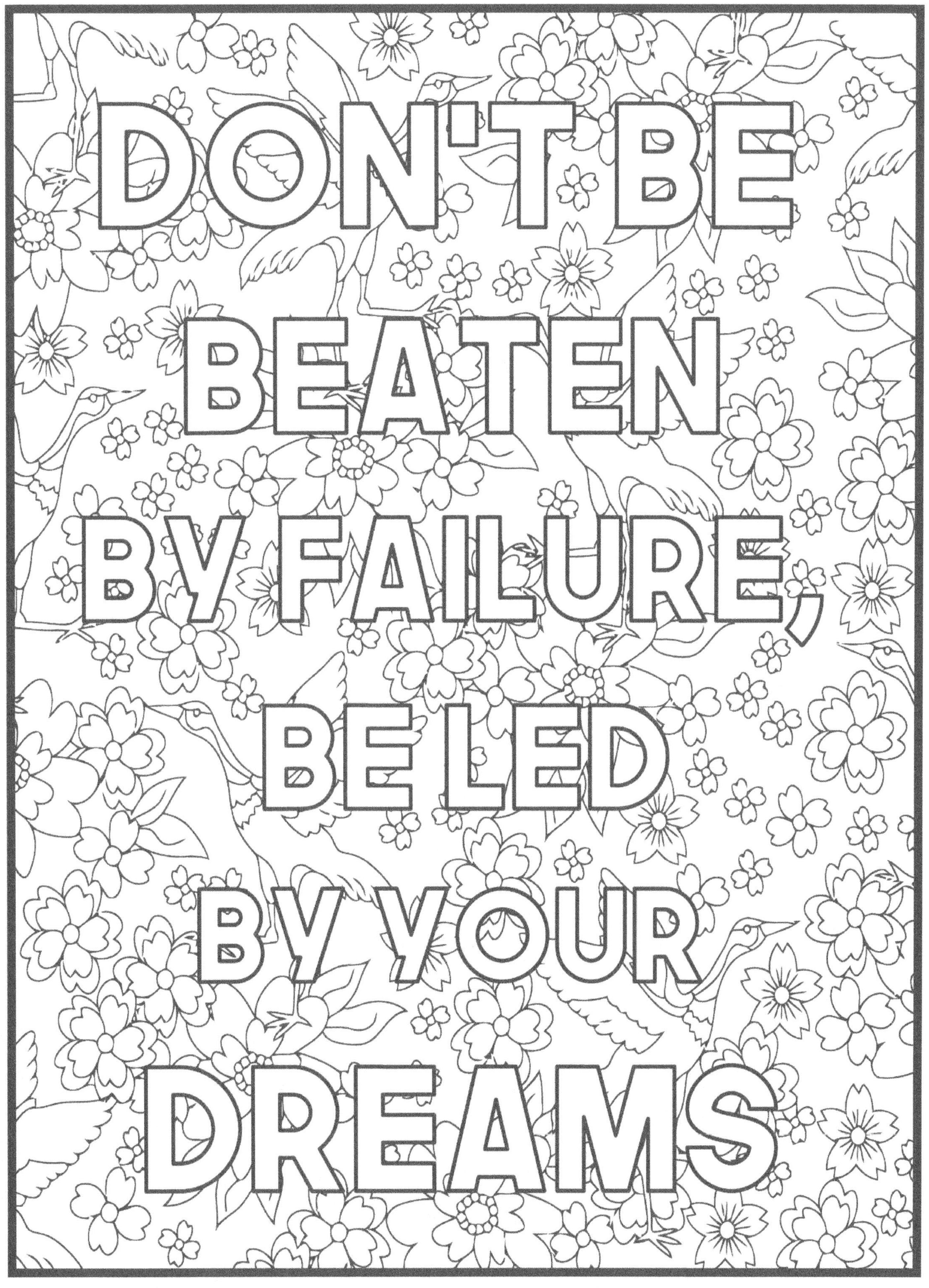

DON'T BE
BEATEN
BY FAILURE,
BE LED
BY YOUR
DREAMS

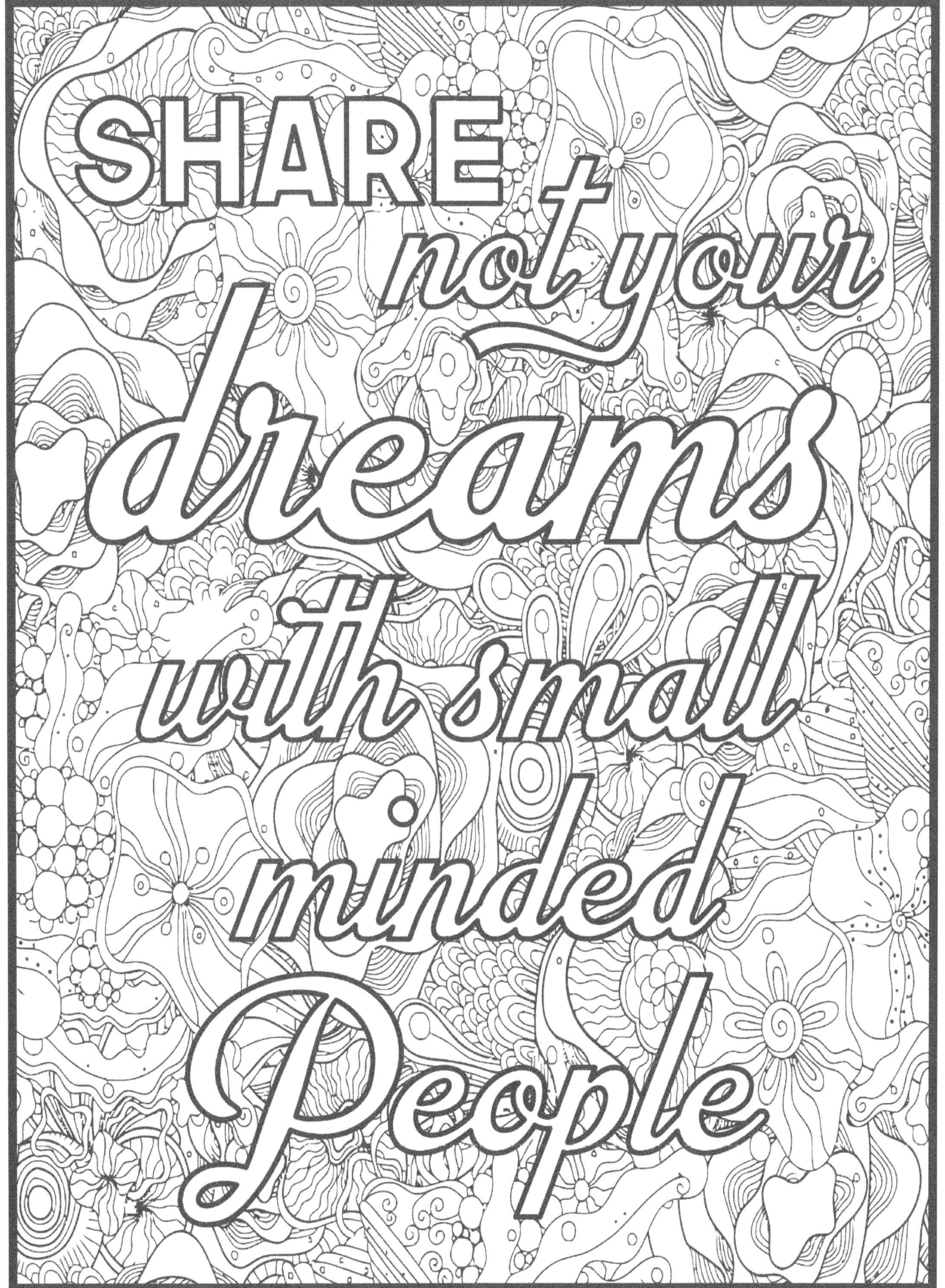

SHARE not your
dreams
with small
minded
People

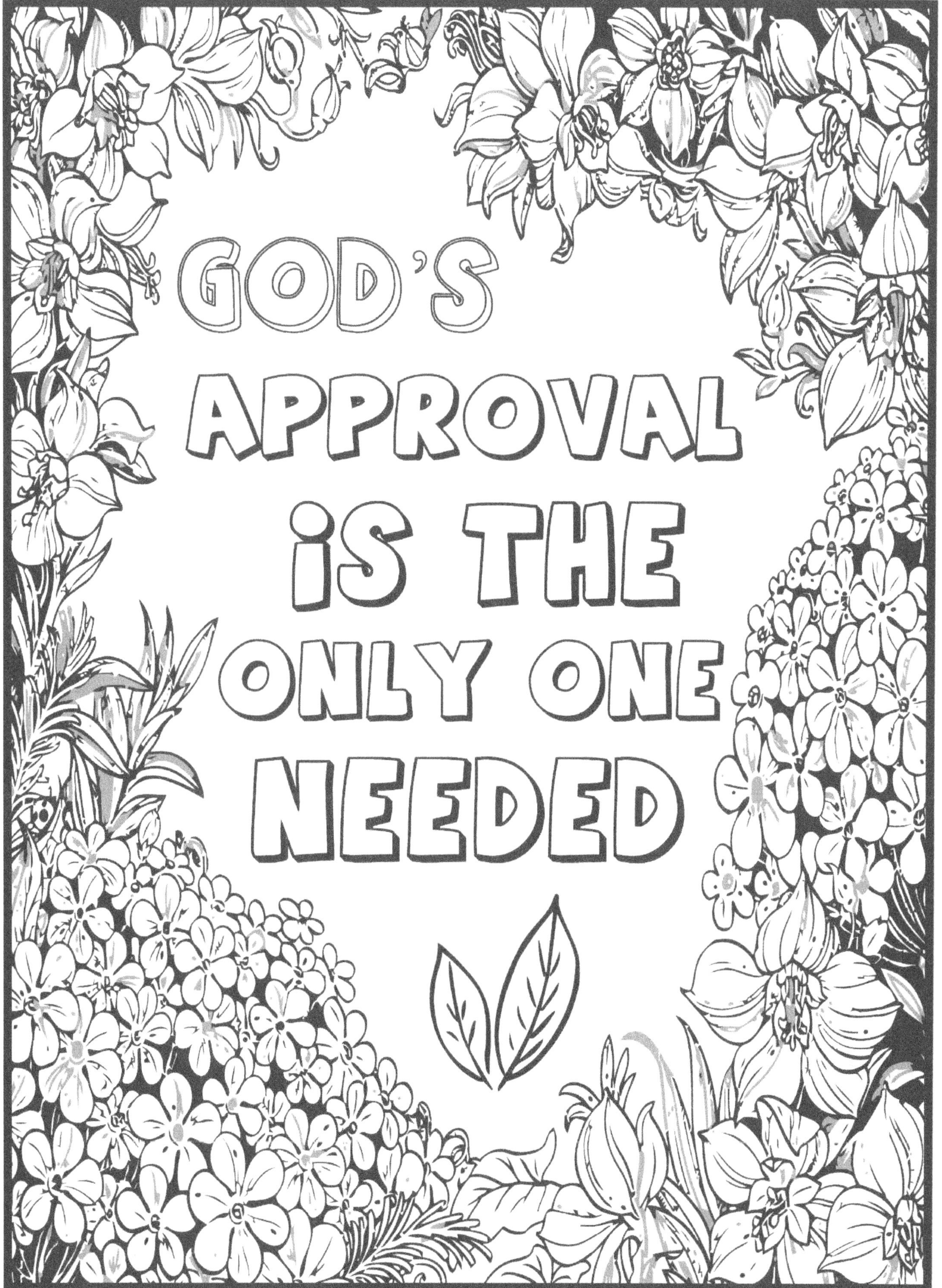
GOD'S
APPROVAL
IS THE
ONLY ONE
NEEDED

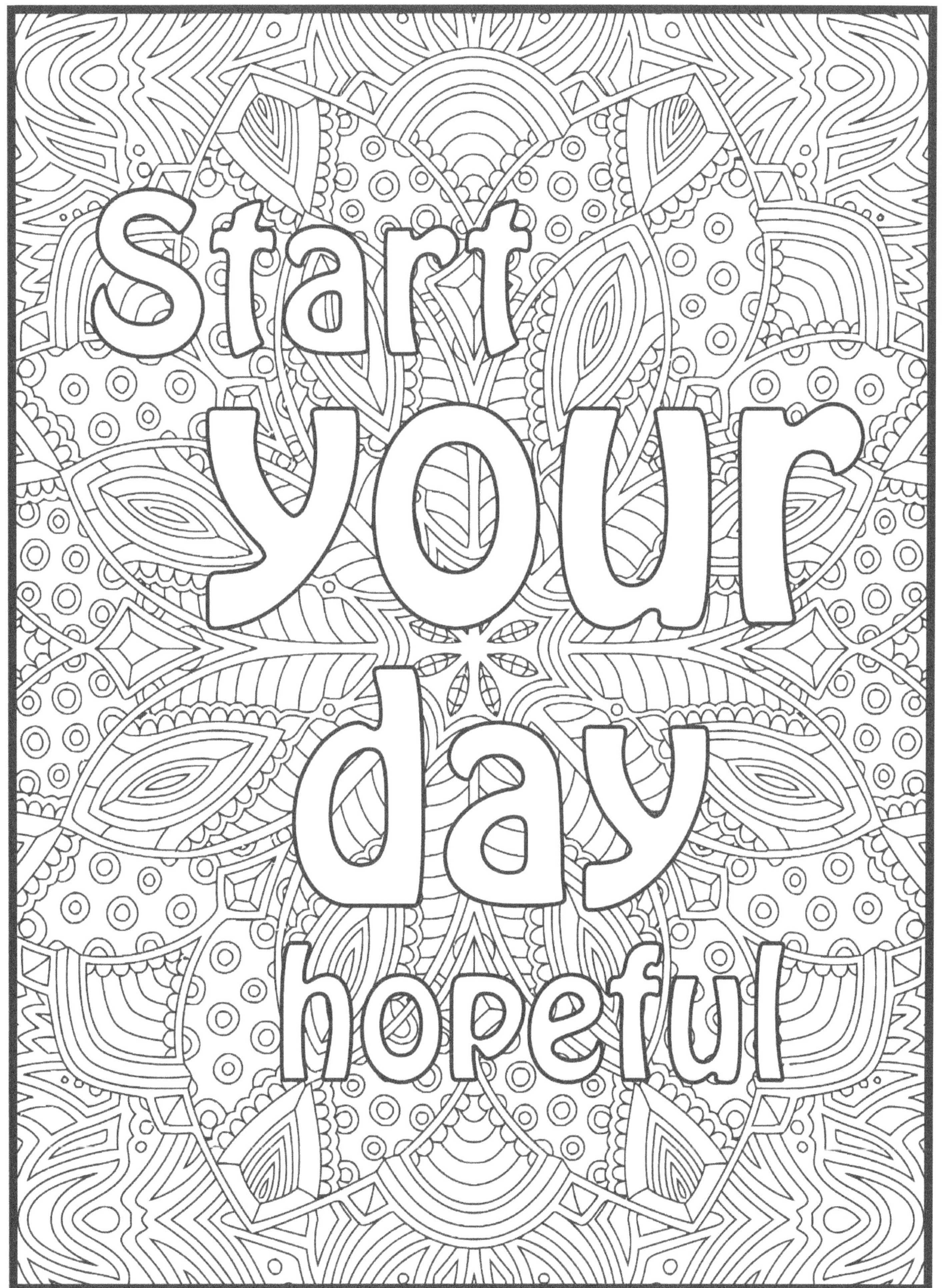

Start
your
day
hopeful

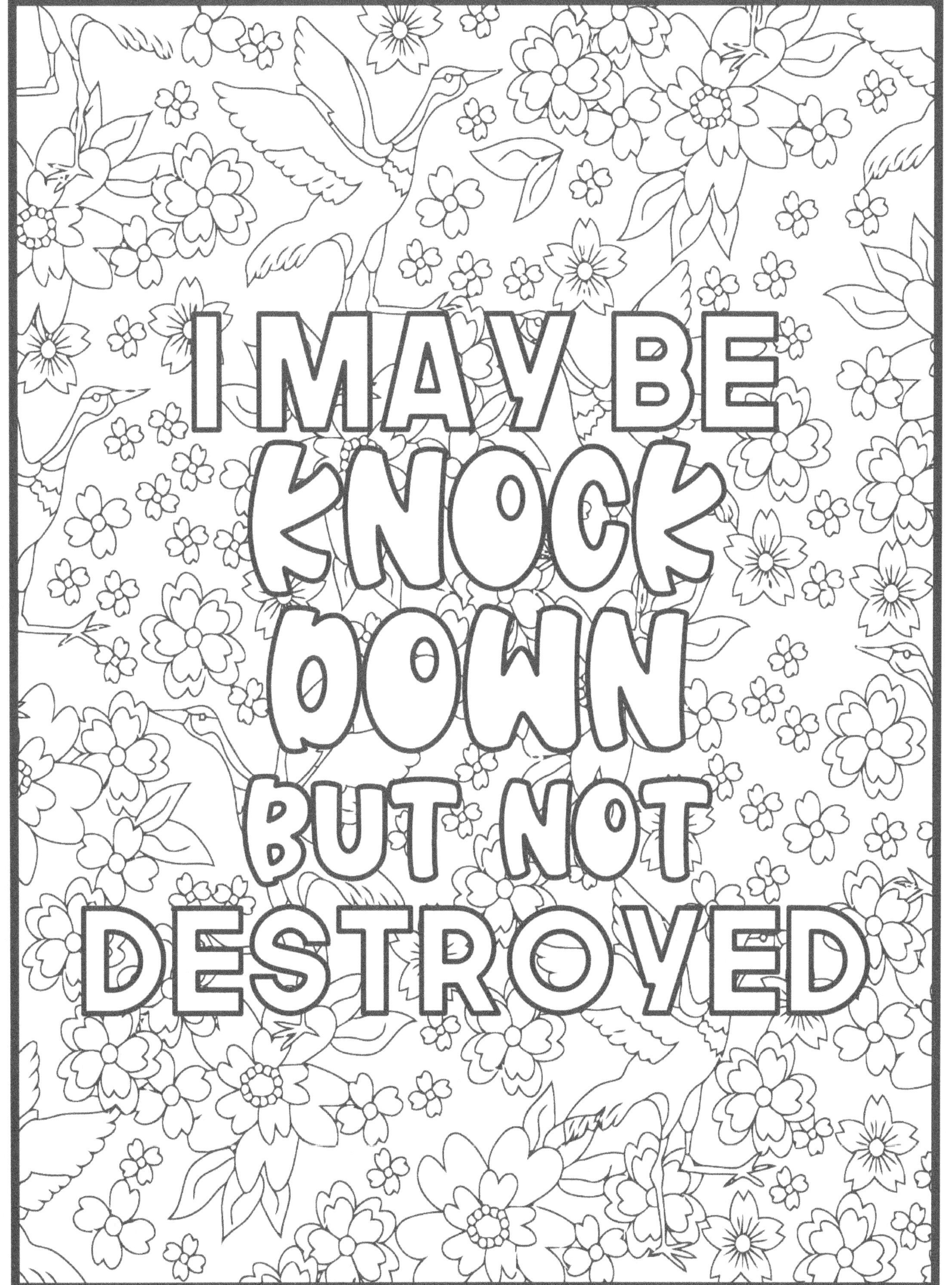

I MAY BE
KNOCK
DOWN
BUT NOT
DESTROYED

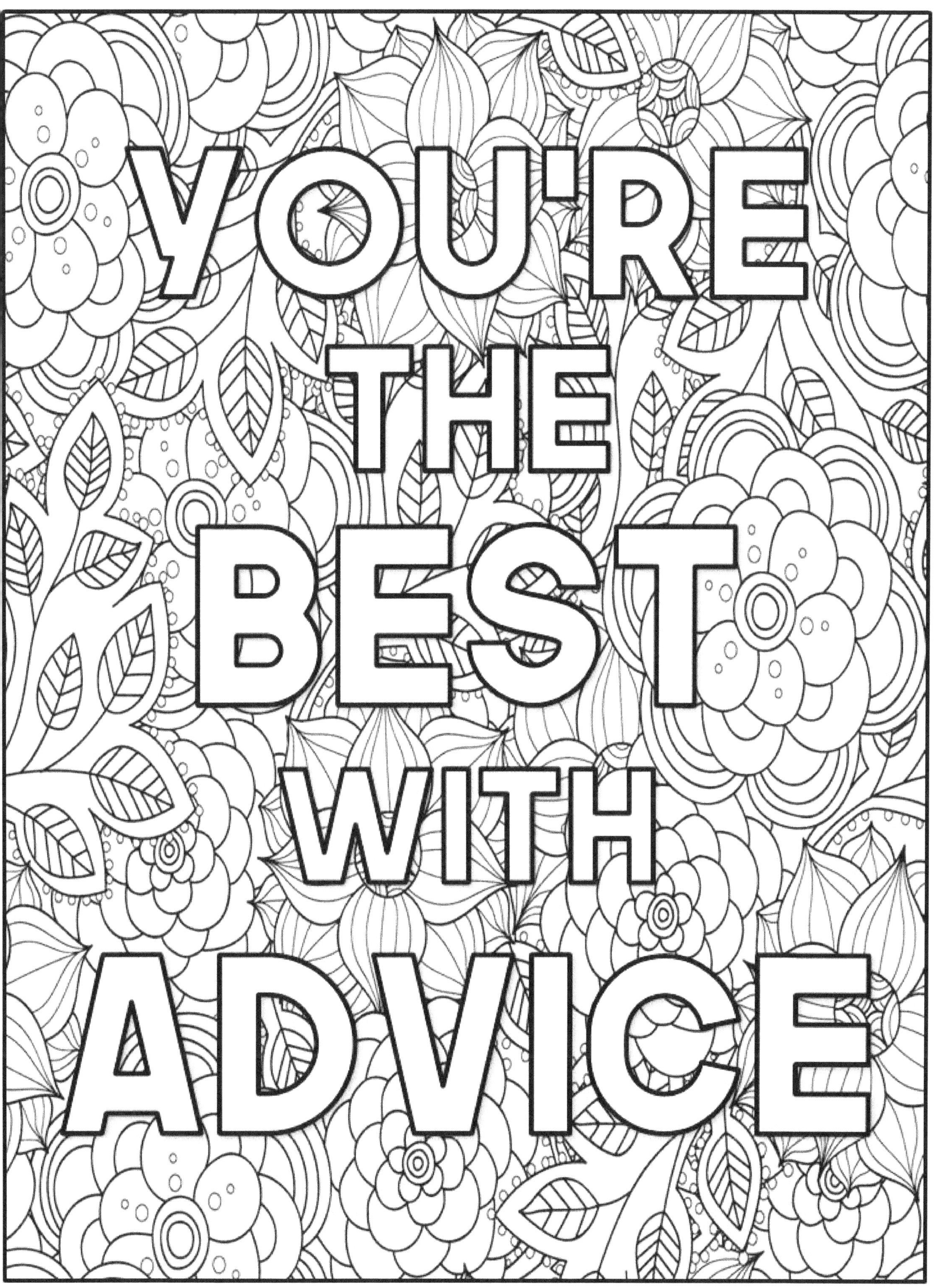
YOU'RE
THE
BEST
WITH
ADVICE

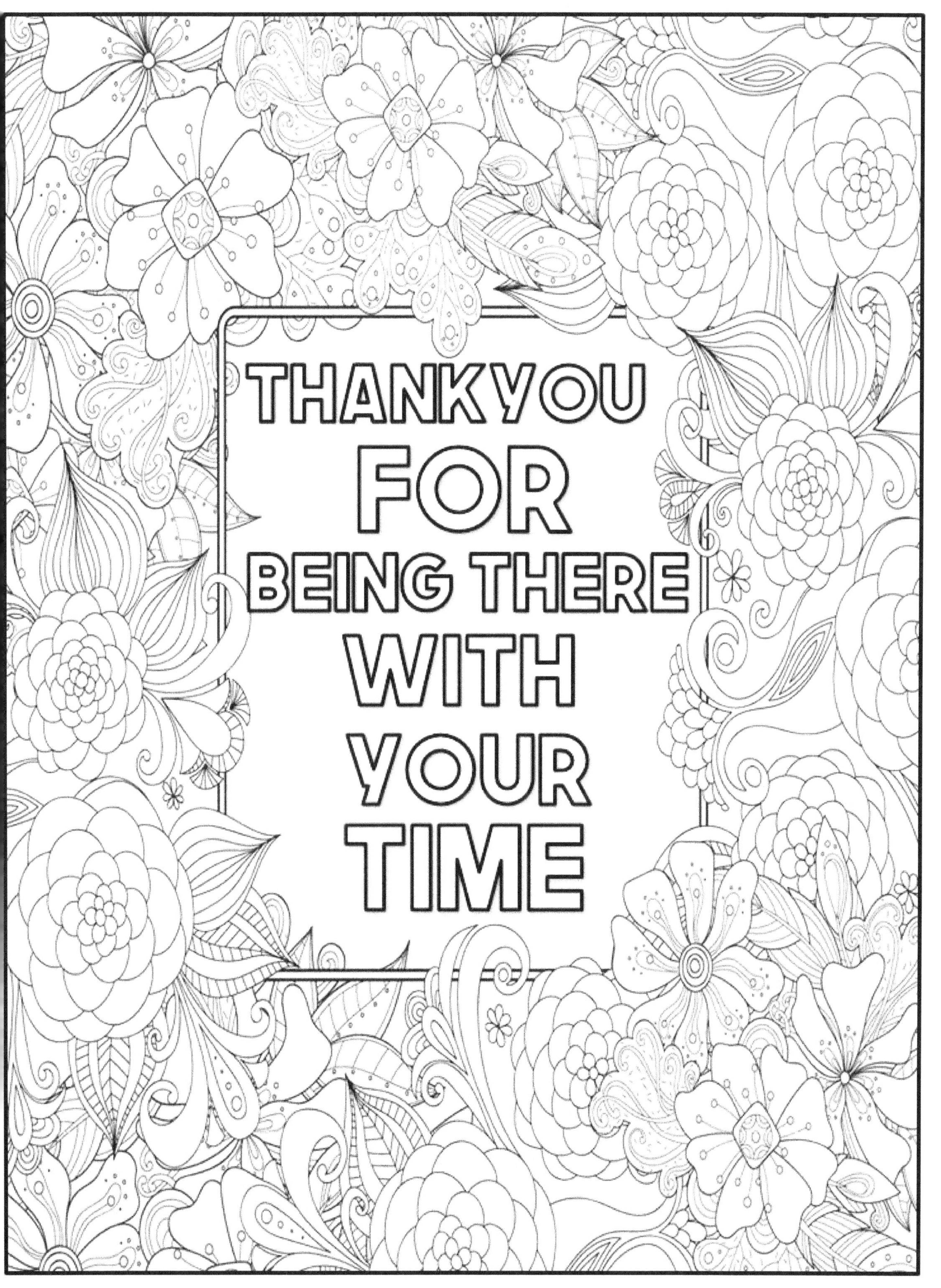
THANKYOU
FOR
BEING THERE
WITH
YOUR
TIME

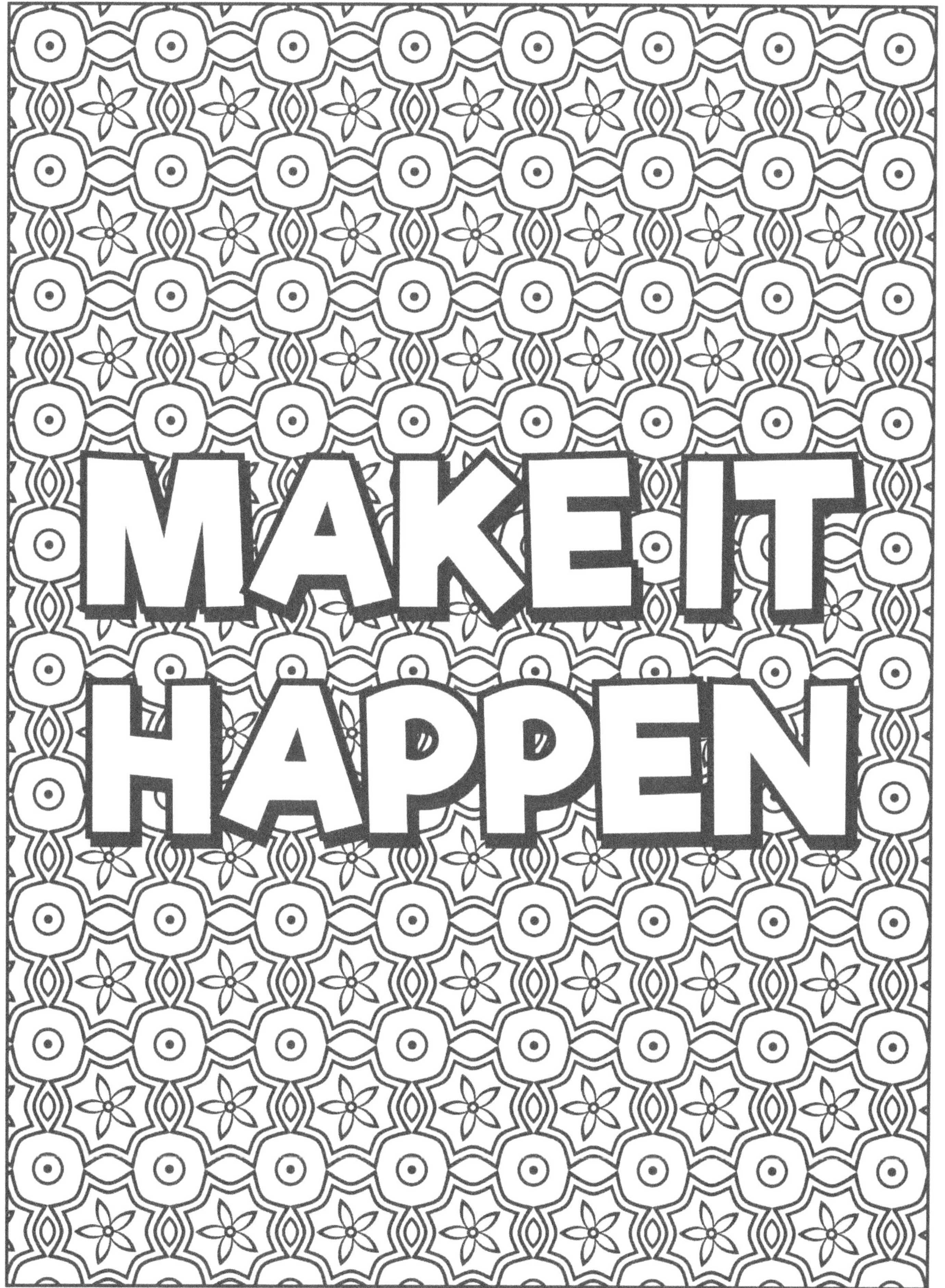

MAKE IT
HAPPEN

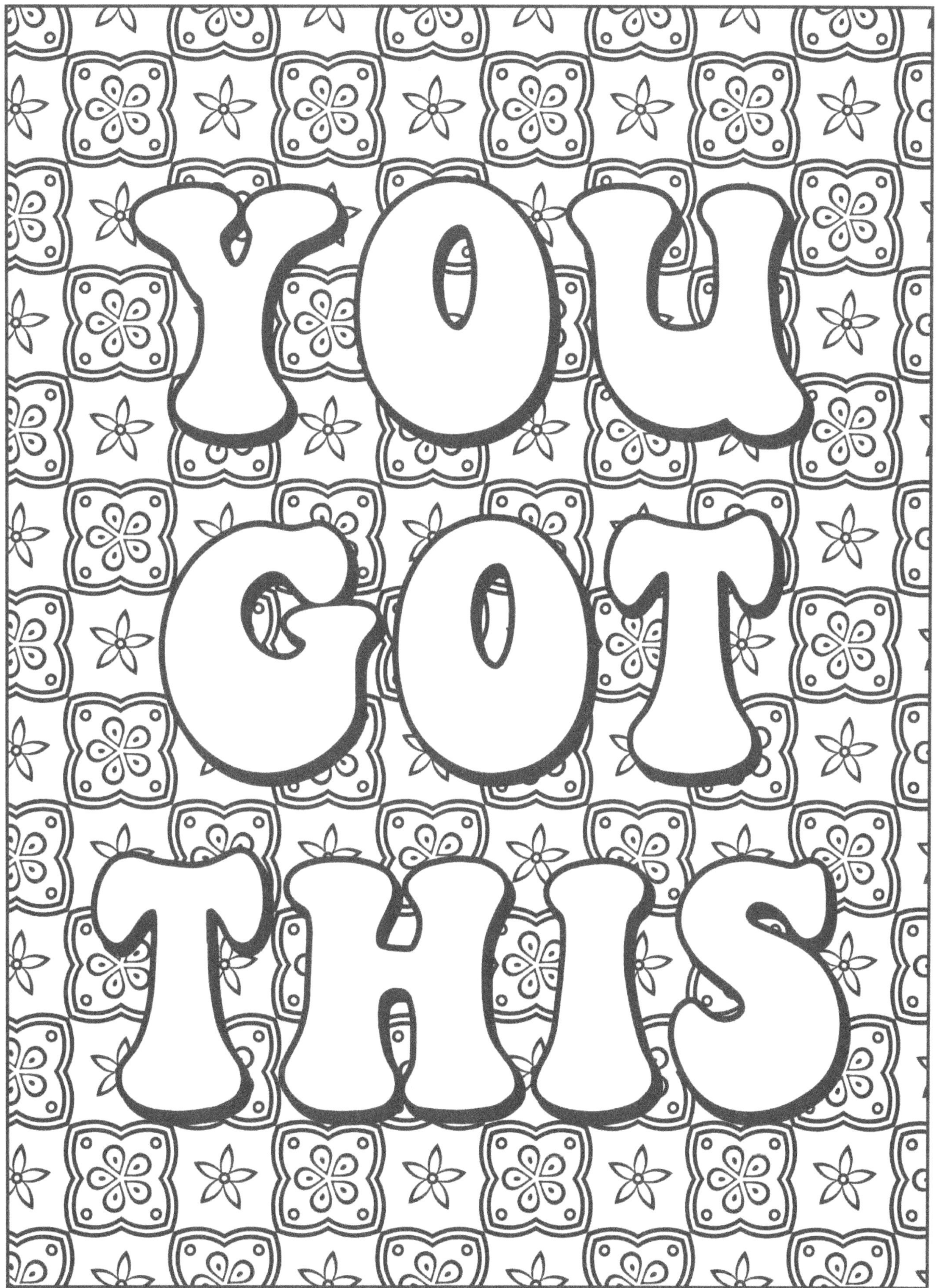

YOU
GOT
THIS

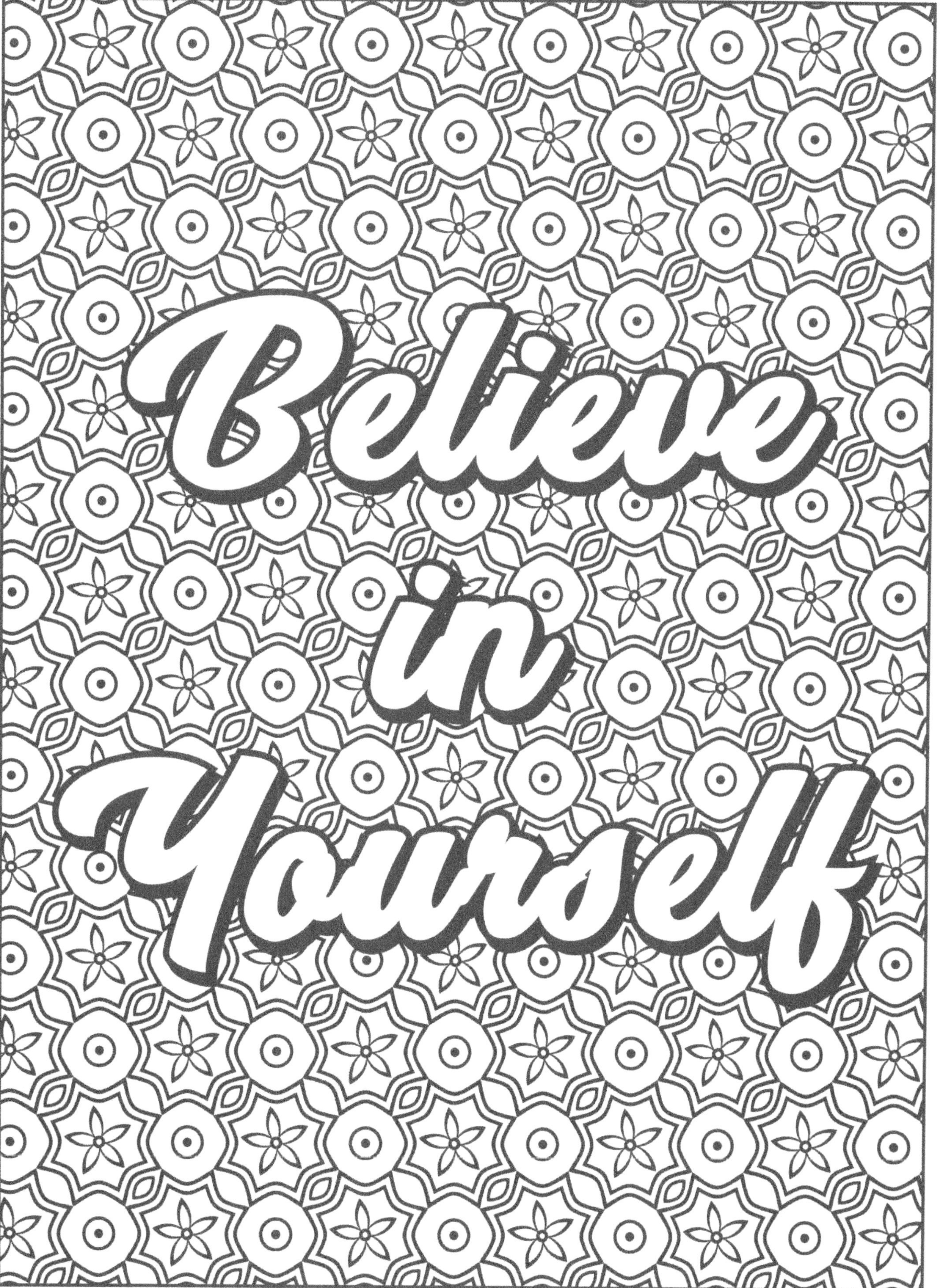

Believe
in
Yourself